## Copyright © 2015 by Connor Taylor

## Disclaimer

I am not a registered dietician or nutritional expert. I enjoy creating delicious milkshakes and the reader should consult a healthcare professional before making any changes to their diet.

# Introduction

In today's society we as a population do not consume enough nutrients within our diet, one drink that rarely comes to mind when someone mentions the word "healthy" is the milkshake. My book is full of 50 delicious milkshake recipes for you to try out at home and is separated into easy to read sections:

- 10 Classic Milkshake Recipes

- 10 Fruit Milkshake Recipes

- 20 Super Milkshake Recipes

- 5 Vegan Milkshake Recipes

- 5 Nutty Milkshake Recipes

This book will encourage you to include more nutritious foods into your diet and in turn will help you to lead a happier and healthier lifestyle. Milkshake making is a fun and fantastic way for children to get involved in healthy eating from a young age! My recipes have been tried and tested at home and perfected for my own taste. Please use my recipes as guidance and feel free to alter any ingredients to your own personal preference.

# The Nutritional Value of Milkshakes

Milkshakes are a great source of nutrition for the following reasons:

- Milk is high in calcium, which is used in the body for strong bone growth and development.

- An aggregate of protein molecules called "whey" can be found in milk, this aggregate aids the body in protein production; a vital process within our bodies.

- Essential fats can be obtained from milk which are used to regulate our core body temperature and acts as an insulator during cold spells.

- Milkshakes contain carbohydrates, more commonly known as sugars. These are used to power our bodily processes such as digestion, neurological processes in the brain and muscle contractions.

- Milkshakes can contain fruits and vegetables which are a fantastic source of vitamins and minerals. Fruits such as mangoes, strawberries and citrus fruits are high in vitamin C which helps to combat diseases.

- Fiber is an extremely important nutrient in our digestive and excretory systems; fiber comes from the fruits and vegetables which can be added to milkshakes.

# 10 CLASSIC MILKSHAKE RECIPES

## Vanilla Shake

**Ingredients:**
- 2 teaspoons vanilla extract
- 3 scoops vanilla ice cream
- 1 pint fresh milk

**How to make this shake:**
1. Using a blender or milkshake machine, blend all ingredients together until smooth.
2. Serve in tall glasses with a straw.
3. Garnish with a fresh strawberry.

# Banana Shake

**Ingredients:**
- 2 bananas
- 3 scoops vanilla ice cream
- 1 pint fresh milk
- 1-2 drops banana essence
- Crystallized banana pieces (for garnishing)

**How to make this shake:**
1.Using a blender or milkshake machine, blend all ingredients together until smooth.
2. Serve in tall glasses with a straw.
3. Garnish with a crystallized banana pieces.

# Strawberry Shake

**Ingredients:**
- 150g fresh strawberries
- 3 scoops vanilla ice cream
- 1 pint fresh milk
- 1 tablespoon strawberry syrup (for garnishing)

**How to make this shake:**
1. Using a blender or milkshake machine, blend all ingredients together until smooth.
2. Serve in tall glasses with a straw.
3. Garnish with a fresh strawberry.

# Chocolate Shake

**Ingredients:**
- 100g grated milk chocolate
- 3 scoops chocolate ice cream
- 1 pint fresh milk
- 1 tablespoon chocolate syrup (for garnishing)

**How to make this shake:**
1. Using a blender or milkshake machine, blend all ingredients together until smooth.
2. Serve in tall glasses with a straw.
3. Garnish with grated milk chocolate and drizzle with chocolate syrup.

# Toffee Shake

**Ingredients:**
- 50g toffee chunks
- 3 scoops vanilla ice cream
- 1 pint fresh milk
- 1 tablespoon toffee syrup (for garnishing)

**How to make this shake:**
1. Using a blender or milkshake machine, blend all ingredients together until smooth.
2. Serve in tall glasses with a straw.
3. Garnish with toffee chunks and drizzle with toffee syrup.

# Mint Choc-Chip Shake

**Ingredients:**
- 50g milk chocolate chips
- 3 scoops mint choc-chip ice cream
- 1 pint fresh milk
- Sprig of fresh mint (for garnishing)

**How to make this shake:**
1. Using a blender or milkshake machine, blend all ingredients together until smooth.
2. Serve in tall glasses with a straw.
3. Garnish with a sprig of fresh mint on top.

# <u>Raspberry Shake</u>

## Ingredients:
- 100g fresh raspberries
- 3 scoops vanilla ice cream
- 1 pint fresh milk - 1 tablespoon raspberry syrup (for garnishing)

## How to make this shake:
1. Using a blender or milkshake machine, blend all ingredients together until smooth.
2. Serve in tall glasses with a straw.
3. Garnish with 1-2 raspberries and drizzle with raspberry syrup.

# **Banoffee Shake**

**Ingredients:**
- 3 scoops vanilla ice cream
- 1 pint fresh milk
- 2 tablespoons banoffee syrup (1 tablespoon for garnishing)

**How to make this shake:**
1. Using a blender or milkshake machine, blend all ingredients together until smooth.
2. Serve in tall glasses with a straw.
3. Garnish by drizzling banoffee syrup on top.

# Peanut Butter Shake

## Ingredients:
- 1 tablespoon peanut butter
- 3 scoops vanilla ice cream
- 1 pint fresh milk
- 2-3 peanuts (for garnishing)

## How to make this shake:
1. Using a blender or milkshake machine, blend all ingredients together until smooth.
2. Serve in tall glasses with a straw.
3. Garnish with whole peanuts on top.

# Chocolate Peanut Butter Shake

**Ingredients:**
- 100g grated milk chocolate
- 3 scoops vanilla ice cream
- 1 pint fresh milk
- 1 tablespoon peanut butter
- 1 tablespoon chocolate syrup (for garnishing)
- 2-3 peanuts (for garnishing)

**How to make this shake:**
1. Using a blender or milkshake machine, blend all ingredients together until smooth.
2. Serve in tall glasses with a straw.
3. Garnish with whole peanuts on top and drizzle with chocolate syrup.

# 10 FRUIT MILKSHAKE RECIPES

# Mango Shake

## Ingredients:
- 1/2 mango chopped into chunks
- 3 scoops vanilla ice cream
- 1 pint fresh milk

## How to make this shake:
1. Using a blender or milkshake machine, blend all ingredients together until smooth.
2. Serve in tall glasses with a straw.

# **Pineapple and Kiwi Shake**

**Ingredients:**
- 2 tinned pineapple slices
- 1/2 kiwi  - 3 scoops vanilla ice cream
- 1 pint fresh milk
- Crystallized pineapple pieces (for garnishing)

**How to make this shake:**
1. Using a blender or milkshake machine, blend all ingredients together until smooth.
2. Serve in tall glasses with a straw.
3. Garnish with crystallized pineapple pieces.

# Blueberry Shake

**Ingredients:**
- 125g fresh blueberries (3 for garnishing)
- 3 scoops vanilla ice cream
- 1 pint fresh milk

**How to make this shake:**
1. Using a blender or milkshake machine, blend all ingredients together until smooth.
2. Serve in tall glasses with a straw.
3. Garnish with 3 blueberries on top.

# Blackberry and Raspberry Shake

**Ingredients:**
- 100g fresh blackberries
- 100g fresh raspberries
- 3 scoops vanilla ice cream
- 1 pint fresh milk

**How to make this shake:**
1. Using a blender or milkshake machine, blend all ingredients together until smooth.
2. Serve in tall glasses with a straw.

# Lemon Shake

## Ingredients:
- 1/2 fresh lemon
- 3 scoops vanilla ice cream
- 1 pint fresh milk
- Lemon syrup (for garnishing)
- Lemon rind (for garnishing)

## How to make this shake:
1. Using a blender or milkshake machine, blend all ingredients together until smooth.
2. Serve in tall glasses with a straw.
3. Garnish with grated lemon rind and drizzle lemon syrup.

# Lime Shake

**Ingredients:**
- 1/2 fresh lime
- 3 scoops vanilla ice cream
- 1 pint fresh milk
- Lime rind (for garnishing)

**How to make this shake:**
1. Using a blender or milkshake machine, blend all ingredients together until smooth.
2. Serve in tall glasses with a straw.
3. Garnish with grated lime rind on top.

# Pear Shake

**Ingredients:**
- 1 tin of pears
- 3 scoops vanilla ice cream
- 1 pint fresh milk
- 1 tablespoon honey
- 1 teaspoon ground nutmeg (for garnishing)

**How to make this shake:**
1. Using a blender or milkshake machine, blend all ingredients together until smooth.
2. Serve in tall glasses with a straw.
3. Garnish with ground nutmeg on top.

# Peach Shake

## Ingredients:
- 1 tin of peaches
- 3 scoops vanilla ice cream
- 1 pint fresh milk
- Sprig of fresh mint (for garnishing)

## How to make this shake:
1. Using a blender or milkshake machine, blend all ingredients together until smooth.
2. Serve in tall glasses with a straw.
3. Garnish with sprig of mint on top.

# Honeydew Melon Shake

**Ingredients:**
- 1/2 honeydew melon
- 3 scoops vanilla ice cream
- 1 pint fresh milk
- 2 tablespoons honey

**How to make this shake:**
1. Using a blender or milkshake machine, blend all ingredients together until smooth.
2. Serve in tall glasses with a straw.

# Cherry Shake

**Ingredients:**
- 50g fresh cherries
- 3 scoops vanilla ice cream
- 1 pint fresh milk
- 1 tablespoon cherry syrup (for garnishing)

**How to make this shake:**
1. Using a blender or milkshake machine, blend all ingredients together until smooth.
2. Serve in tall glasses with a straw.
3. Garnish with cherry syrup.

# 20 SUPER MILKSHAKE RECIPES

## Spinach and Mint Shake

**Ingredients:**
- 100g fresh baby spinach
- 3 scoops vanilla ice cream
- 1 pint fresh milk
- 25g fresh mint
- Sprig of fresh mint (for garnishing)

**How to make this shake:**
1. Using a blender or milkshake machine, blend all ingredients together until smooth.
2. Serve in tall glasses with a straw.
3. Garnish with sprig of mint on top.

# Avocado and Banana Shake

**Ingredients:**
- 1 avocado
- 1 banana
- 3 scoops vanilla ice cream
- 1 pint fresh milk

**How to make this shake:**
1. Using a blender or milkshake machine, blend all ingredients together until smooth.
2. Serve in tall glasses with a straw.

# Banana and Chia Seed Shake

## Ingredients:
- 1 banana
- 3 scoops vanilla ice cream
- 1 pint fresh milk
- 50g chia seeds

## How to make this shake:
1. Using a blender or milkshake machine, blend all ingredients together until smooth.
2. Serve in tall glasses with a straw.

# Coffee Shake

### Ingredients:
- 1 teaspoon instant coffee
- 3 scoops vanilla ice cream
- 1 pint fresh milk
- 1 tablespoon chocolate syrup (for garnishing)

### How to make this shake:
1. Using a blender or milkshake machine, blend all ingredients together until smooth.
2. Serve in tall glasses with a straw.
3. Garnish with chocolate syrup.

# Banana and Mint Choc-Chip Shake

## Ingredients:
- 1 banana
- 50g chocolate chips
- 3 scoops mint choc-chip ice cream
- 1 pint fresh milk

## How to make this shake:
1. Using a blender or milkshake machine, blend all ingredients together until smooth.
2. Serve in tall glasses with a straw.

# **Apple and Cinnamon Shake**

## **Ingredients:**
- 1 apple
- 3 scoops vanilla ice cream
- 1 pint fresh milk
- 1 teaspoon cinnamon
- 1 tablespoon apple syrup (for garnishing)

## **How to make this shake:**
1. Using a blender or milkshake machine, blend all ingredients together until smooth.
2. Serve in tall glasses with a straw.
3. Garnish with apple syrup.

# Flaxseed Shake

## Ingredients:
- 50g flaxseed
- 50g oats (leave some for garnishing)
- 3 scoops vanilla ice cream
- 1 pint fresh milk
- 2 tablespoons honey

## How to make this shake:
1. Using a blender or milkshake machine, blend all ingredients together until smooth.
2. Serve in tall glasses with a straw.
3. Garnish with oats on top.

# **Strawberry and Lime Shake**

## **Ingredients:**
- 100g fresh strawberries
- 1/2 lime
- 3 scoops of vanilla ice cream
- 1 pint of fresh milk
- 1 tablespoon strawberry syrup

## **How to make this shake:**
1. Using a blender or milkshake machine, blend all ingredients together until smooth.
 2. Serve in tall glasses with a straw.
3. Garnish with strawberry syrup.

# <u>Marshmallow Shake</u>

## Ingredients:
- 5 marshmallows (2 for garnishing)
- 3 scoops vanilla ice cream
- 1 pint fresh milk
- 1 tablespoon chocolate syrup

## How to make this shake:
1. Using a blender or milkshake machine, blend all ingredients together until smooth.
2. Serve in tall glasses with a straw.
3. Garnish with chocolate syrup and marshmallows on top.

# Chilli and Chocolate Shake

**Ingredients:**
- 1/2 teaspoon crushed chilli flakes
- 100g grated milk chocolate
- 3 scoops vanilla ice cream
- 1 pint fresh milk

**How to make this shake:**
1. Using a blender or milkshake machine, blend all ingredients together until smooth.
2. Serve in tall glasses with a straw.

# Banana and Chilli Shake

## Ingredients:
- 1 banana
- 1/2 teaspoon crushed chilli flakes
- 3 scoops vanilla ice cream
- 1 pint fresh milk
- Crystallized banana pieces (for garnishing)

## How to make this shake:
1. Using a blender or milkshake machine, blend all ingredients together until smooth.
2. Serve in tall glasses with a straw.
3. Garnish with banana pieces on top.

# Banana and Ginger Shake

**Ingredients:**
- 1 banana
- 1/2 teaspoon grated ginger
- 3 scoops vanilla ice cream
- 1 pint fresh milk

**How to make this shake:**
1. Using a blender or milkshake machine, blend all ingredients together until smooth.
2. Serve in tall glasses with a straw.

# Vanilla and Chilli Shake

## Ingredients:
- 2 teaspoons vanilla extract
- 1/2 teaspoon crushed chilli flakes
- 3 scoops vanilla ice cream
- 1 pint fresh milk

## How to make this shake:
1. Using a blender or milkshake machine, blend all ingredients together until smooth.
2. Serve in tall glasses with a straw.

# Citrus Shake

## Ingredients:
- 1/2 fresh lemon
- 1/2 fresh lime
- 3 scoops vanilla ice cream
- 1 pint fresh milk
- 1/2 teaspoon grated lemon rind (for garnishing)
- 1/3 teaspoon grated lime rind (for garnishing)

## How to make this shake:
1. Using a blender or milkshake machine, blend all ingredients together until smooth.
2. Serve in tall glasses with a straw.
3. Garnish with rind of lemon and lime on top.

# **Pumpkin Shake**

## **Ingredients:**
- 1 tablespoon pumpkin puree
- 1/2 teaspoon cinnamon
- 3 scoops vanilla ice cream
- 1 pint fresh milk
- 3-4 pumpkin seeds (for garnishing)

## **How to make this shake:**
1. Using a blender or milkshake machine, blend all ingredients together until smooth.
2. Serve in tall glasses with a straw.
3. Garnish with pumpkin seeds.

# Dark Chocolate and Chilli Shake

## Ingredients:
- 100g dark chocolate chopped into chunks
- 1/2 teaspoon crushed chilli flakes
- 3 scoops vanilla ice cream
- 1 pint chocolate milk
- 1 tablespoon chocolate syrup (for garnishing)

## How to make this shake:
1. Using a blender or milkshake machine, blend all ingredients together until smooth.
2. Serve in tall glasses with a straw.
3. Garnish with chocolate syrup.

# White Chocolate Shake

### Ingredients:
- 100g white chocolate chopped into chunks
- 3 scoops vanilla ice cream
- 1 pint fresh milk
- 1 tablespoon chocolate syrup

### How to make this shake:
1. Using a blender or milkshake machine, blend all ingredients together until smooth.
2. Serve in tall glasses with a straw.
3. Garnish with chocolate syrup.

# White Chocolate and Raspberry Shake

## Ingredients:
- 100g white chocolate chopped into chunks
- 125g fresh raspberries
- 3 scoops vanilla ice cream
- 1 pint fresh milk

## How to make this shake:
1. Using a blender or milkshake machine, blend all ingredients together until smooth.
2. Serve in tall glasses with a straw.
3. Garnish with raspberry syrup.

# **Coconut Shake**

### **Ingredients:**
- 3 scoops vanilla ice cream
- 1 pint coconut milk
- 1 strawberry (for garnishing)

### **How to make this shake:**
1. Using a blender or milkshake machine, blend all ingredients together until smooth.
2. Serve in tall glasses with a straw.
3. Garnish with fresh strawberry.

# Cherry and Dark Chocolate Shake

**Ingredients:**
- 50ml cherry liqueur
- 100g dark chocolate chopped into chunks
- 3 scoops vanilla ice cream
- 3/4 pint fresh milk
- 1 tablespoon cherry syrup (for garnishing)

**How to make this shake:**
1. Using a blender or milkshake machine, blend all ingredients together until smooth.
2. Serve in tall glasses with a straw.
3. Garnish with cherry syrup.

# 5 VEGAN MILKSHAKE RECIPES

## Vegan Banana and Peanut Butter Shake

**Ingredients:**
- 1 banana
- 2 tablespoons peanut butter
- 5 ice cubes
- 1 pint almond milk
- 2-3 peanuts (for garnishing)

**How to make this shake:**
1. Using a blender or milkshake machine, blend all ingredients together until smooth.
2. Serve in tall glasses with a straw.
3. Garnish with whole peanuts on top.

# Vegan Chocolate Shake

**Ingredients:**
- 1 banana
- 2 tablespoons cacao powder
- 1 pint soya chocolate milk
- 5 ice cubes

**How to make this shake:**
1. Using a blender or milkshake machine, blend all ingredients together until smooth.
2. Serve in tall glasses with a straw.

# Vegan Berry Shake

## Ingredients:
- 100g fresh strawberries (1 for garnishing)
- 100g fresh raspberries
- 1 pint soya milk
- 5 ice cubes

## How to make this shake:
1. Using a blender or milkshake machine, blend all ingredients together until smooth.
2. Serve in tall glasses with a straw.
3. Garnish with fresh strawberry.

# Vegan Almond Shake

## Ingredients:
- 1 banana
- 2 tablespoons almond butter
- 1 pint almond milk
- 5 ice cubes
- 2-3 almonds (for garnishing)

## How to make this shake:
1. Using a blender or milkshake machine, blend all ingredients together until smooth.
2. Serve in tall glasses with a straw.
3. Garnish with almonds on top.

# **<u>Vegan Berry Shake</u>**

## **Ingredients:**
- 125g frozen blueberries
- 100g frozen blackberries
- 1 pint soya milk
- 5 ice cubes

## **How to make this shake:**
1. Using a blender or milkshake machine, blend all ingredients together until smooth.
2. Serve in tall glasses with a straw.

# 5 NUTTY MILKSHAKE RECIPES

## Hazelnut Shake

**Ingredients:**
- 50g chopped hazelnuts
- 3 scoops vanilla ice cream
- 1 pint hazelnut milk
- 1 tablespoon toffee syrup (for garnishing)

**How to make this shake:**
1. Using a blender or milkshake machine, blend all ingredients together until smooth.
2. Serve in tall glasses with a straw.
3. Garnish with toffee syrup.

# Brazil Nut Shake

**Ingredients:**
- 50g chopped brazil nuts
- 3 scoops vanilla ice cream
- 1 pint chocolate milk
- Sprig of mint (for garnishing)

**How to make this shake:**
1. Using a blender or milkshake machine, blend all ingredients together until smooth.
2. Serve in tall glasses with a straw.
3. Garnish with sprig of mint on top.

# Almond Shake

## Ingredients:
- 50g chopped almonds
- 3 scoops vanilla ice cream
- 1 mint almond milk
- 1 tablespoon toffee syrup (for garnishing)

## How to make this shake:
1. Using a blender or milkshake machine, blend all ingredients together until smooth.
2. Serve in tall glasses with a straw.
3. Garnish with toffee syrup.

# Pistachio Shake

**Ingredients:**
- 4 tablespoons blanched, peeled and ground pistachios
- 1 tablespoon sugar
- 1 pint fresh milk
- 5 ice cubes

**How to make this shake:**
1. Using a blender or milkshake machine, blend all ingredients together until smooth.
2. Serve in tall glasses with a straw.

# Banana and Walnut Shake

**Ingredients:**
- 1 banana
- 50g chopped walnuts (2-3 for garnishing)
- 3 scoops vanilla ice cream
- 1 pint fresh milk

**How to make this shake:**
1. Using a blender or milkshake machine, blend all ingredients together until smooth.
2. Serve in tall glasses with a straw.
3. Garnish with walnuts on top.

Thank you for reading my book and I hope you enjoyed making my 50 homemade milkshake recipes,

Connor

13006323R00032

Printed in Poland
by Amazon Fulfillment
Poland Sp. z o.o., Wrocław